# IMPULSE BALANCE THEORY AND IST EXTENSION BY AN ADDITIONAL CRITERION CORRECTED VERSION BY

## Reinhard Selten

Königswinter, Germany

April 2015

www.ProfessorSelten.com
Info@ProfessorSelten.com

# IMPULSE BALANCE THEORY
## Abstract

In this paper I present a description of the theory of impulse Balance. This theory predicts a mixed strategy for every player in an arbitrary n-person game in normal form. However, this mixed strategy is not interpreted as the result of a process of rational deliberation, but rather the behavioral distribution of pure strategies in a long section of a supergame of the normal form game. As the length of the section moves to infinity, the process of pure strategy choice approaches a stationary state with fixed mixed strategies attached to it. This is the basic idea guiding our theory construction. The theory has been first developed as a concept for $2 \times 2$ – games only (Selten and Chmura AER 2008). The theory can be easily generalized to normal forms with more than two pure strategies for some players. In the paper by Selten and Chmura a number of theories have been compared with experimental data on repeated $2 \times 2$ - games with anonymous interaction and changing opponents from one game to the next in the comparison the quadratic deviation between theoretical predictions and data is lowest for impulse balance theory. This was a surprising success of impulse balance theory. In a paper by Chmura, Goerg and Selten the theory of impulse balance is generalized to arbitrary normal forms. This paper also presents a learning model whose stationary distributions of pure strategies are impulse balance solutions and vice versa. The learning model opens the way for numerical computation of impulse balance predictions. Moreover the Chmura, Goerg and Selten paper also reports experimental data on a specific class of $3 \times 3$ – games (the class of bailiff and poacher games, see Selten. R., Anticipatory learning in n-person games, in: Game equilibrium models 1, Reinhard Selten (ed.) in Springer Verlag Berlin – Heidelberg –New York 1991). In the class of bailiff and poacher games every game has a unique Nash equilibrium and also a unique impulse balance solution. Therefore this class is well suited for the comparison of both concepts. The experiments on $3 \times 3$ – games reported in the paper by Chmura, Goerg, and Selten have been run on 12 games with completely mixed Nash equilibria and 14 games with partially mixed Nash equilibria. Nash equilibrium and impulse balance theory are both parameter free concepts which unlike most other concepts do not depend on parameters which have to be estimated from the experimental data and are not available before an experiment is run. Theories which are not parameter free in this sense are not truly predictive. The quadratic distance from the data is usually much smaller for impulse balance theory, than for Nash equilibrium. Impulse balance is clearly more successful in this comparison between the two parameter free theories. In a business problem not directly treatable by impulse balance the theory can be applied nevertheless with the help of an additional criterion 70% correct long term predictions of the future distribution of decision behavior were obtained in first experiments.

Keywords: impulse balance, Nash equilibrium, bailiff and poacher games.

## Table of Contents

ABSTRACT ......................................................................................................... - 2 -

1 INTRODUCTION ............................................................................................ - 4 -

2 PRELIMINARY DEFINITION AND NOTATIONS ................................................ - 4 -

3 BAILIFF AND POACHER GAMES ..................................................................... - 5 -

4 NORMAL FORMS WITHOUT AND WITH RANDOM INFLUENCES ..................... - 6 -

    4.1. THE PURE STRATEGY SET VECTOR ........................................................ - 6 -

    4.2. THE PAYOFF VECTOR FUNCTION .......................................................... - 7 -

5 THE IMPULSE CONCEPT ............................................................................... - 10 -

6 THE GENERALIZED IMPULSE BALANCE THEORY ........................................... - 12 -

7 ADDITIONAL CRITERION THEORY - IMPULSE BALANCE THEORY WITH AN ADDITIONAL CRITERION GIVES IN EXPERIMENTS ON A BUSINESS PROBLEM ABOUT 70% CORRECT LONG TERM PREDICTIONS. ........................................................................................ - 13 -

8 NASH-EQUILIBRIA OF BAILIFF AND POACHER GAMES ................................... - 14 -

9 SUMMARY AND CONCLUSION ..................................................................... - 16 -

REFERENCES ................................................................................................... - 18 -

# 1 Introduction

Here we first deal with the 3 × 3 – game experiments from the paper by Chmura, Goerg and Selten. It is convenient to repeat some passages from the introduction to this earlier paper without any change. The predominance of behavioral concepts in terms of descriptive success over Nash equilibrium is a well – documented fact. Regularly, behavioral concepts describe the data gathered in laboratory experiments much better than the Nash equilibrium does. Such behavioral concepts are, for example, new stationary concepts (e.g., MacKelevey and Palfrey, 1995, 1998; Selten and Chmura, 2008; Goerg and Selten, 2009), models of level – thinking (e.g., Nagel 1995; Ho *et al.*, 1998; Crawford and Costa – Gomes, 2006), and models describing learning a processes (e.g. Roth and Erev, 1995; Erev and Roth, 1998; *et al.*, 2007; Chmura *et al.* 2012)[1].

One stationary alternative that performed significantly better in previous studies than Nash equilibrium is impulse balance theory (Selten and Chmura, 2008). It is a non – parametric concept based on the idea of learning direction theory (Selten and Buchta, 1999). Probabilities of decision are modeled as behavioral tendencies and adjusted similar to the adjustments of a marksman aiming at a trunk: "*If he misses the trunk to the right, he will shift the position of the bow to the left and if he misses the trunk to the left he will shift the position of the bow to the right. The marksman looks at his experience from the last trial and adjusts his behavior [...]*" (p.86, Selten and Buchta, 1999). There is no need for further adjustments when a stationary state is reached.

In previous studies impulse balance was first applied to auctions (Selten *et al.*, 2005; Okenfels and Selten, 2005) and later on to 2 × 2 games (Avrahami el al., 2005; Selten and Chmura, 2008), 2 × 2 × 2 games (Avrahami el al., 2005), as well as cyclic games (Goerg and Selten, 2009). In addition to out – performing Nash, impulse balance theory, performed at least as good as quantal response equilibrium in 2 × 2 games. Although quantal response equilibrium is a parametric concept and impulse balance theory is not (Selten and Chmura, 2008; Brunner et al., 2011).

# 2 Preliminary definition and notations

Up to now impulse balance theory was only applied to games in which players had two pure strategies as decision alternatives to choose from. In this paper now, we introduced a generalized version of impulse balance theory, which can be applied to any normal form game. The predictive power of generalized impulse balance is then tested against the one of Nash equilibrium, the experiments are based on the *Bailiff and Poacher Games* (Selten, 1991). In total we gathered data on 26 games, 12 games with completely mixed Nash equilibria and 14 with partial mixed strategies. Impulses over optimistically are based on the

---

[1] In Ho *et al. (2007)* self – tuning experience –weighted attraction learning competes against quantal response equilibrium, which is a harder competitor than Nash.

best payoff against $\pi_{-i}^{t-1}$. Therefore the double counting of losses in judging a period's success makes sense.

In section 3, we compare the performances of generalized impulse balance and Nash over all 26 experimental bailiff and poacher games, within the two classes of games with completely mixed and partially mixed Nash equilibria.

## 3. Bailiff and poacher games

Bailiff and poacher games are special bimatrix games. The bimatrix is shown in figure 1.

|  |  | Poacher's choice | | |
|---|---|---|---|---|
|  |  | 1 | 2 | 3 |
| Balliff's choice | 1 | 1 / 0 | 0 / $V_2$ | 0 / $V_3$ |
|  | 2 | 0 / $V_1$ | 1 / 0 | 1 / $V_3$ |
|  | 3 | 0 / $V_1$ | 0 / $V_2$ | 1 / 0 |

*Figure 1: Bailiff and poacher games.*

Figure 1 shows the bailiff and poacher games. The normal forms games depend on three parameters $V_1, V_2, V_3$. The parameters have the meaning of the poacher's attraction to stealing from the three ponds 1, 2 and 3 respectively. If the bailiff watches pond $i$, he can only watch one of the $ponds$ every day. If the poacher is caught he receives $zero$ payoffs and the bailiff gets payoff 1. If the poacher choses another strategy $j$ $with$ $j \neq i$ he succeeds in stealing fish from pond $j$ and receives the payoff $V_j$ and the bailiff receives payoff $zero$.

The game of figure 1 is not the bailiff and poacher game described by Selten (1991), but a different game, which however, lends itself to an interpretation by the same story. This game is used in the paper by Chmura, Goerg and Selten and is also described here as the normal form of the class of Bailiff and poacher games. The games of Selten in 1999 turned out to be too difficult to analyze with respect to the Nash equilibrium and therefore has been replaced by the game of figure 1 which is quite different but the same story as in the original game lends itself to the interpretation of figure 1.

## 4 Normal forms without and with random influences

A normal form with or without random influences: $G = (\Pi, H)$ has the following constituents:

1) A pure strategy set vector and
2) A vector payoff function.

We shall now describe the two constituents in more detail and begin with 1) the pure strategy set vector.

### 4.1 The pure strategy set vector

$$\Pi = (\Pi_1, \ldots, \Pi_n) \text{ or } \hat{\Pi} = (\Pi_0, \ldots, \Pi_n)$$

The strategy sets $\Pi_i$ are non-empty and finite sets of objects called pure strategies.

The set $\Pi_0$, if it is present, is a set of random influences $\pi_0 \in \Pi_0$, which occur with fixed probabilities $p_0(\pi_0)$.

$p_0$ is a probability distribution over $\Pi_0$, i.e. we have:

$$p_0(\pi_0) \geq 0 \; and \sum_{\pi_0 \in \Pi_0} p_0(\pi_0) = 1$$

The Players $1, \ldots, n$ are called personal players.

At the beginning of the game every personal player $i$ selects a pure strategy $\pi_i \in \Pi_i$. This results in a combination:

$$\pi = (\pi_1, \ldots, \pi_n)$$

of pure strategies with

$$\pi_i \in \Pi_i \quad for \quad i = 1, \ldots, n$$

In a normal form with random influences in addition to this a random strategy $\pi_0 \in \Pi_0$ is drawn from $\Pi_0$ and this together with $\pi$ yields an extended combination

$$\hat{\pi} = (\pi_0, \pi_1, \ldots, \pi_n)$$

Note that only one $\pi_0$ appears in every extended pure strategy combination $\hat{\pi}$. In forming the probability of $\hat{\pi}$ the probability $p_0(\pi_0)$ is applied to the combination

$$\pi = (\pi_1, \ldots, \pi_n)$$

as a whole and not to the components $\pi_i$ separately.

A mixed strategy $q_i$ for a personal player $i$ is a probability distribution over $\Pi_i$. The set of all mixed strategies of player $i$ is denoted by $Q_i$.

We also consider combinations of mixed strategies

$$q = (q_1, \ldots, q_n) \quad \text{with} \quad q_i \in Q_i$$

We use the notation $\hat{\pi} = \pi_0 \pi$ in order to express the relationship between $\hat{\pi}$ and $\pi$ and $\pi_0$ in normal forms with random influences.

We regard a pure strategy $\pi_i$ as a special mixed strategy $q_i$

$$\text{with} \quad q_i(\pi_i) = 1$$
$$\text{and} \quad q_i(\varrho_i) = 0 \quad \text{for } \varrho_i \neq \pi_i$$

for every other pure strategy $\varrho_i$ with $\varrho_i \neq \pi_i$

## 4.2 The payoff vector function

In normal forms without random influences the payoff vector function $h_i$ is always defined on the set $K(\Pi)$, the set of all pure combinations

$$\pi = (\pi_1, \ldots, \pi_n)$$

which can result from the selection of

$$\pi_i \; from \; \Pi_i \quad for \; i = 1, \ldots, n$$

for normal forms with random influences $\hat{\Pi}$, the set of all extended combinations $\hat{\pi} = \pi_0 \pi$ which can be formed by a selection of $\hat{\pi} = \pi_0 \pi$ from the components of $\hat{\Pi}$. This set denoted by $K(\hat{\Pi})$ is called the set of extended pure combinations. For normal forms with random influences we use the notation:

$$\hat{\pi} = \pi_0 \pi \quad with \; \pi_0 \in \Pi_0 \quad and \; \pi \in K(\Pi)$$

In this way we express the relationships among $\hat{\pi}$, $\pi$, and $\pi_0$.

A mixed strategy $q_i$ for personal player $i$ is a probability distribution over $\Pi_i$. We regard a pure strategy $\pi_i$ as a special mixed strategy $q_i$:

$$with \; q_i(\pi_i) = 1 \quad and \quad q_i(\varrho_i) = 0 \quad for \; every \quad \varrho_i \in \Pi_i \; with \; \varrho_i \neq \pi_i$$

A combination of mixed strategies $q = (q_1, \ldots, q_n)$ contains a mixed strategy $q_i$ for every personal player $i$.

We shall also look at extended mixed combinations:

$$\hat{q} = p_0(q_1, \ldots, q_n) = p_0 q$$

$$\hat{q} = p_0(\pi_0) q \quad in \; analogy \; to \quad \hat{\pi} = p_0(\pi_0) \pi$$

It must be pointed out there is in only one $\pi_0$ in every extended mixed combination. Only one $\pi_0$ is used in $p_0(\pi_0)$ for all personal players.

The random influences are the same ones for every player $1, \ldots, n$ and do not depend on the pure strategy combinations, selected in the game. In the game random influences are "neutral" and do not favor or disfavor anybody $K(\hat{Q})$ is the set of all extended mixed combinations, which can be formed with $p_0$ and $q \in Q$. Here $Q = (Q_1, \ldots, Q_n)$ is the mixed strategy set vector and $Q_i$ is the set of all mixed strategies of player $i$, $(i = 1, \ldots, n)$

Let

$$\hat{q} = p_0(q_1, \ldots, q_n) = p_0 q$$

be an extended combination of mixed strategies with the probability that $\hat{q}$ results in an extended pure strategy combination

$$\hat{\pi} = (\pi_0, \pi_1, \ldots, \pi_n)$$

This probability is:

$$\hat{q}(\hat{\pi}) = p_0(\pi_0) \times q_1(\pi_1) \times, \ldots, \times q_n(\pi_n)$$

The product of the factors:

$$q_1(\pi_1), \ldots, q_n(\pi_n)$$

can also be expressed as follows:

$$q_1(\pi_1) \times \ldots \times q_n(\pi_n) = \text{Prod} \quad q_i(\pi_i)$$
$$i = 1, \ldots, n$$
$$\pi_i \in \Pi_i$$

The symbol *Prod* means that the product of all expressions following *Prod* under the conditions noted below *Prod* is to be formed. An example:

$$\text{Prod} \quad i^2 \qquad = 1 \times 4 \times 9 = 36$$
$$i = 1, 2, 3$$

The probability of:

$$\hat{\pi} = p_0(\pi_0), (\pi_1, \ldots, \pi_n) \quad \text{is}$$
$$\hat{q}(\hat{\pi}) = p_0(\pi_0) \times \text{Prod} \qquad q_i(\pi_i)$$
$$\pi_i \in \Pi_i$$
$$i = 1, \ldots, n$$

Expected payoff :

The expected payoff vector $for$ $q = (q_1, \ldots, q_n)$ $is$

$$H(q) = (H_1(q), \ldots, H_n(q))$$

The components are

$$H_i(q) = p_0(\pi_0) \times \text{Prod} \quad q_i(\pi_i)$$
$$i = 1, \ldots, n$$
$$\pi_i \in \Pi_i$$

## 5 The Impulse concept

Consider a personal $player\ i$, who has just observed a combination

$$\pi^{t-1} = (\pi_1^{t-1}, \ldots, \pi_n^{t-1})$$

in a normal form without random influences. An $i - incomplete$ combination

$$\pi_i = (\pi_1, \ldots, \pi_{i-1}, \pi_{i+1}, \ldots, \pi_n)$$

Is an $(n-1) - tuple$ containing a pure strategy $\pi_j$ for every personal $player\ j\ with\ j \neq i$.

We use the notation $\quad \pi = \pi_i \pi_{-i}$

$Define \quad r(\pi_{-i}) = \max h_i(\varrho_i \pi_{-i})$
$\quad \varrho_i \in \Pi_i$

$$r_i(\pi_{-i}^{t-1}) = \max \quad h_i(\varrho_i \pi_{-i}^{t-1})$$
$$\varrho_i \in \Pi_i$$

The special $\varrho_i$ which maximizes the right hand side of this equation is called the ex post maximizer of $r_i(\pi_{-i}^{t-1})$ $of\ player\ i$ against $\pi_{-i}^{t-1}$.

The impulse experienced by *player i* by observing
$$\pi_{-i}^{t-1} = (\pi_1^{t-1},\ldots,\pi_{i-1}^{t-1},\pi_{i+1}^{t-1},\ldots,\pi_n^{t-1}) \text{ is the difference}$$

$$imp_i(\pi^{t-1}) = r_i(\pi_{-i}^{t-1}) - h_i(\pi^{t-1})$$

Let $r_i(\pi_{-i}^{t-1})$ is the maximal payoff *player i* could have received by choosing the ex post maximizer of $r_i(\pi_{-i}^{t-1})$ of *player i* instead of $\pi_i^{t-1}$

*Player i* may be attracted to the ex post maximizer
$$\varrho_i \text{ of } h_i(\varrho_i \pi_{-i}^{t-1}).$$

The impulse
$$imp_i(\pi^{t-1}) = r_i(\varrho_i \pi_{-i}^{t-1}) - h_i(\pi_i^{t-1},\pi_{-i}^{t-1})$$

Is the maximal additional amount *player i* could have got in in period $t-1$ by $\varrho_i$ instead of $\pi_i^{t-1}$.

We assume that this ex post maximizer influences the mixed strategy $\omega_i^t$ which describes *player i's* pure strategy choice in period $t$

$$w_i^t = \frac{t-1}{t}\pi_i^{t-1} + \frac{1}{t}\varrho_i^{t-1}$$

for the average of all $w_i^t$ of participants within a fixed interaction group k. A stationary state maybe reached in different interaction groups at different time points.

Let $w_i^t$ and $w_i^{t+1}$ be values of $w_i$ for the same interaction group $k$. $w_i^t$ being stationary in a sequence $T_S = t, t+1,\ldots, T-1, T$ in this interaction group means that

$$w_i^{t+1} = w_i^t \qquad for\ t\ \epsilon\ T_s$$

holds everywhere in $T_s$. Let $|T_s|$ be the length $T - t$ of such at sequence $T_s$.

We denote this length by $|T_s|$. The theory of impulse balance proceeds from the assumption that the sequence $w_t, \ldots$ becomes more and more similar to a stationary sequence as $|T_s|$ approaches infinity. This can be proved for special environments, but there is no guarantee, that this will always happen. If we look at sequences

$$T_s \text{ with } |T_s| = L \text{ and with } L \to \infty$$

It may happen that never a stationary state is reached, but the system always cycles around a stationary state. One can show for special environments that we have convergence to the property of $w^t$ being stationary and thereby show that convergence to being stationary for $|T_s| \to \infty$ is not impossible. However, this will not be done here.

## 6 The Generalized impulse balance theory

In impulse balance theory we assume that such a stationary state is more and more approached in a play.

Impulse balance is nothing else than the description off such a state and how it is reached. It is of course possible that in some cases repeated play of the same normal form does not converge in this way. We exclude this by assumption on the normal form. Assume that in period $t-1$ used strategy combination:

$$\pi^{t-1} \in K(\Pi)$$

has been played. What is then experience of $player\ i$ in the preceding period $t-1$ and what is then the pure strategy $\pi_i^t$ for period $t$ which then emerges in response. This question will now be explored and answers will be given by the theory of impulse balance. Let as first look at the basis, on which it is decided whether the choice of $\pi_i^{t-1}$ in the preceding period $t-1$ resulted in a gain or a loss. For this purpose we look at the maximum with respect to $\varrho_i$ of the minimum with respect to $\pi_{-i}$ of $h_i(\varrho_i\,\pi_{-i})$.

Define

$$s_i = \max_{\varrho_i \in \Pi_i} \min_{\pi_{-i} \in K(\Pi_i)} h_i(\varrho_i\,\pi_{-i})$$

$s_i$ is the pure strategy maximin, the maximal payoff obtainable if the worst happens with respect to the joint $i-$ incomplete strategy combination

$$\pi_{-i} = (\pi_1, \ldots, \pi_{i-1}, \pi_{i+1}, \ldots, \pi_n)$$

We also refer to $s_i$ as security level of $player\ i$. A strategy $\varrho_i$ which maximizes the right hand side of the equation for $s_i$ is called a maximin strategy of $player\ i$.

# 7 Additional criterion theory - Impulse balance theory with an additional criterion gives in first experiments on a business problem about 70% correct long term predictions.

After my discovery of impulse balance theory in 2005 I together with various co-authors we have analyzed a number of economic models with the help of this method and we obtained good results. We applied the theory in a number of experimental-studies.

In year 2012 I discovered a relatively complex business problem which is not directly treatable by impulse balance. Nevertheless it can be treated with the theory and the help of an **additional criterion**.

In complex business problems one can obtain good predictions of long run decision behavior (up to 70% correct predictions in the evaluation of the first experiment).

The **additional criterion** excludes decisions in certain situations in days, months or longtime periods. The decisions to be made are changes of policy, we shall look at problems of order acceptance. A firm can accept two categories of orders A or B. In this situation there are three possible policies:

    1 (accept only orders A)
    2 (accept only orders B)
    3 (accept orders A and B)

If the firm accepts the order it cannot accept any other orders for a number of periods. We refer to this number as the full occupation time (f.o.t.). The f.o.t. is 4 periods for orders of type A and 2 periods for orders of type B. The firm receives a profit $P_A = 50$ for an order of type A and $P_B = 10$ for an order of type B. The probability that an order of type A is available in Period t is $w_A = 0.1$ and the probability of an order of type B is 0.2. The probability of at least 2 orders of types A and B is $w_{AB} = 0.05$. The three policies available are:

$\pi_1$: $accept\ only\ orders\ A$

$\pi_2$: $accept\ only\ orders\ B$

$\pi_3$: $accept\ orders\ A\ and\ B\ but\ preferably\ A$

A decision point is a time t at which orders of both categories are available and the firm is not in one of its f.o.t.. A policy can be only changed at a decision point. A decision section is a sequence of consecutive periods

$t_1, t_{1+1}, \ldots, t_{2-1}, t_2.$ , where $t_1\ and\ t_2$ are decision points not falling in a f.o.t. If in a decision section $\pi_1$ has been used but a greater profit sum would have been achieved with $\pi_2$ instead of $\pi_1$ then the firm changes its policy from $\pi_1$ to $\pi_2$. The policy change goes always in the direction of higher profitability if it occurs at all.

# 8 Nash-equilibria of bailiff and poacher games

Bailiff and poacher games are special bimatrix games.

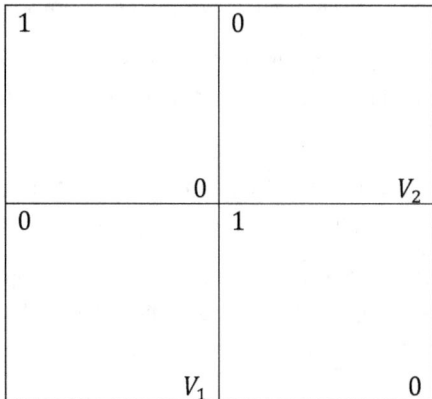

Figure 2: The restricted games for player 1 and player 2 – The North-west subbimatrix of the matrix of figure 1

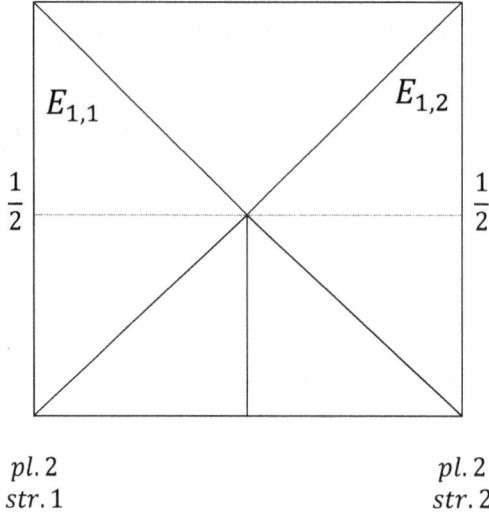

Figure 3: The payoff of player 1

$E_{i,j}$ is the payoff of *player i* for his pure strategy $j$ at full Nash equilibrium, the payoffs of the pure strategies of player 1 in the completely mixed equilibrium $E_{1,1}$ *and* $E_{1,2}$.

We shall now look at the question under which conditions an equilibrium exists, in which the choice 3 is not taken. If such an equilibrium exists it must also be an equilibrium of the subbimatrix of figure 3.

Therefore we now determine the mixed equilibrium of this subbimatrix. Let $E_{i,j}$ be the payoff of *player i* for his or her pure strategy $j$. Figure 3 shows the payoffs $E_{1,1}$ and $E_{1,2}$ as functions of $q_{22}$. The mixed strategy component $q_{22}$ of player 2's mixed strategy

$$q_2 = (q_{21}, q_{22}).$$

We have

$$E_{11} = p_{11}q_{11} \text{ and}$$
$$E_{12} = p_{22}q_{22}$$

At equilibrium we must have $\quad E_{11} = E_{12} = \frac{1}{2}$

Equilibrium is reached at the intersection point of the lines $E_{11}$ and $E_{12}$. There we have

$$E_{11} = E_{12} = \frac{1}{2}$$

It follows that always the equation

$$q_1 = q_2 = \frac{1}{2}$$

must hold.

This equilibrium is an equilibrium of the whole game if and only if the choice 3 yields a lower payoff against

$$p = \left(\frac{1}{2}, \frac{1}{2}\right) \text{ and}$$
$$q = \left(\frac{1}{2}, \frac{1}{2}\right)$$

A similar figure as figure 3 can be drawn in order to represent the payoffs $E_{21}$ and $E_{22}$. This yields in the strategy $q$ in the second equation above.

Inspection of *figure* 1 yields

$$V_3 \le \frac{1}{2}$$

Since, if *player* 1 and *player* 2 use their strategies 1 and 2 with probabilities $\frac{1}{2}$ it follows that each of the fields $i,j$ of figure 1 with $i,j = 1,2$ is reached with probability $\frac{1}{4}$.

Therefore the third field 1,3 or 2,3 must be reached with probability $\frac{1}{2}$. It follows that the expected payoff of player 3 for his strategy 3 if the other players use their strategies with probability $\frac{1}{2}$ is $\frac{V_3}{2}$. If player 1 would also use strategy $q = \left(\frac{q_1}{2}, \frac{q_2}{2}\right)$ he would get and expected payoff of at most $\frac{V_1}{4}$ or $\frac{V_2}{4}$.

In view of $V_1 > V_2 > V_3$ this is more than $\frac{V_3}{2}$. It follows that there cannot be a completely mixed equilibrium of the game of figure 1, unless we have $V_3 \ge \frac{1}{2}$.

Every game in this class involves two players, a bailiff who has to watch one of three ponds, in order to prevent thefts of fish, and a poacher who can try to steal fish from one of the three ponds. The bailiff can only watch one pond on every day and the poacher can only try to steal from one pond every day. The three symbols $V_1, V_2$ and $V_3$ denote the poacher attractions to ponds 1, 2, and 3, resp.. The poacher attractions $V_1, V_2$ and $V_3$ are the values of a theft from pond 1, 2 and 3 resp. for the poacher. We always assume $V_1 > V_2 > V_3$. Apart from the requirement that the poacher attractions of any two ponds are different, this entails no restriction of generality. The inequality can always s be restored by renumbering the players.

## 9 Summary and conclusion

The theory of impulse balance has been described and compared with the concept of Nash equilibrium in a sample of 26 bailiff and poacher games. Each of these games has a unique Nash equilibrium point and a unique impulse balance solution. Therefore the sample lends itself to a comparison of the Nash equilibrium and impulse balance theory. The probabilities from the corresponding relative frequencies in the experimental data defined in a straightforward way as the square of the Euclidean distance between theoretical equilibrium and experimentally observed relative frequencies in altogether 52 interaction groups are much greater for Nash equilibrium than for the impulse balance solution. The difference is shown graphically by figure 4.

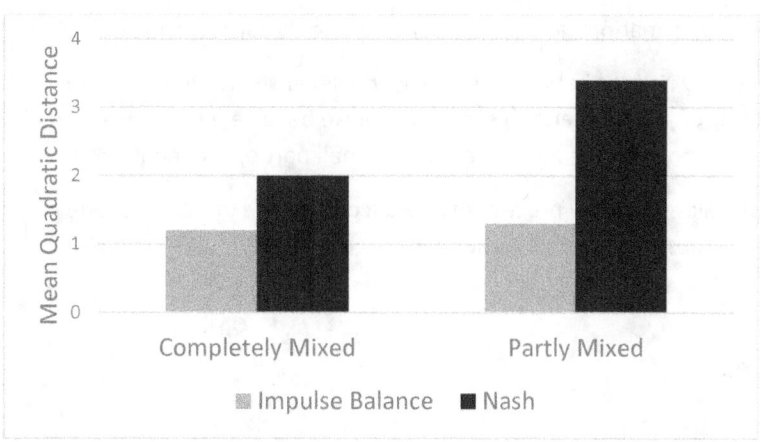

*Figure 4: Squares of distances from data for the subsamples of the games with completely and partly mixed Nash equilibria and for the concepts of Nash equilibrium (black bars) and impulse balance solution (grey bars)*

Our sample of 26 games contains 12 games with completely mixed Nash equilibria and 14 games with partially mixed ones in which strategy 3 is not used at equilibrium, neither by $player$ 1 nor by $player$ 2. The bars in the figure show the sum of quadratic distances for the concept under consideration and the subsample of the 12 games with completely mixed Nash equilibria and of the remaining 14 games (the two bars on the right).

It can be seen that regardless whether we look at the 12 games with completely mixed Nash equilibria or the 14 games with partial Nash equilibria, only.

The impulse balance prediction has a considerably higher success rate and the difference is particularly striking in the case of the subsample of the games with only partial Nash equilibria. The predictive success is the greater the smaller the bar is. In Nash equilibrium is connected to considerably higher bars then the impulse balance solution.

The figure reveals that the better performance of impulse balance is driven by the subsample of the 14 games with partial equilibria only. Some of the squared distances of the theoretical predicted probabilities for the corresponding relative frequencies is are 2.55 times greater for Nash equilibria than for impulse balance in the individual games of the subsample with partial Nash equilibrium, due to the fact that subjects often choose show their strategy 3 in these cases despite of the fact that this is not compatible with equilibrium behavior.

It is also interesting to observe that the predictive success of impulse balance solution does not vary a lot between the subsamples of 12 and 14. For all but four of the observed games the difference is highly significant for the data of single games ($p < 0.01$) for two sided fisher-pitman permutation test replicates.

Based on data from each game separately (see the paper by Chmura, Goerg, Selten. P. 16 Table 3) impulse balance looks only at what have been best given the strategy of the other player of the preceding period.

In this way the information gained by experience is only superficially evaluated.

It is of course very risky to behave in this way, however the riskiness is reduced by the double counting of all losses and this makes impulse balance a quite successful behavior in spite of its failure to evaluate more than a very small part of the feedback information.

If the impulse balance theory proceeds to be successful in experiments, one has to look at the theoretical question why this is the case.

## References

Chmura, T., Georg, S., J., Selten, R., 2013: Generalized Impulse Balance: An Experimental Test for a Class of 3 X 3 Games. Review of Behavioral Economics. 1: 27-53.

McKelvey, R., D., & T., R., Palfrey (1995) "Quantal response equilibria for normal form games." Games an Economic Behaviour, Vol. 10, No. 1, pp. 6-38.

McKelvey, R., & T., Palfrey (1998) "Quantal Response Equilibria for Extensive Form Games", Experimental Economics, Vol. 1, pp. 9-41.

Selten, R., & T., Chmura (2008) "Stationary Concepts for Experimental 2 x 2-Games." The American Economic Review, Vol. 93, No. 3, pp. 938-966.

Goerg, S., J., & R., Selten (2009) "Experimental Investigation of Stationary Concepts in Cyclic Duopoly Games." Experimental Economics, Vol. 12, No. 3, pp. 253-271.

Nagel, R., (1995) "Unraveling in Guessing Games: An Experimental Study", American Economic Review, Vol. 85, No. 5, pp. 1313-1326.

Ho, T., H., Camerer, C., & Weigelt, K., (1998) „Iterated Dominance an Iterated Best Response in Experimental P-Beauty Contests", The American Economic Review, Vol. 88, 947-969.

Crawford, V., P., & M., A., Costa-Gomes (2006) "Cognition and Behavior in Two-Person Guessing Games: An Experimental Study", American Economic Review, Vol. 96, No. 5, pp. 1737-1768.

Roth, A., E., & I., Erev (1995) "Learning in Extensive-Form Games : Experimental Data an Simple Dynamic Models in the Intermediate Term." Games an Economic Behavior, Vol. 8, pp. 164-212.

Erev, I., & A.E., Roth (1998) "Predicting How People Play Games: Reinforcement Learning in Experimental Games with Unique Mixed Strategy Equilibria." American Economic Review, Vol. 88, No. , pp.848-81.

Ho, T., H., Camerer, C., & Chong, J., K., (2007) "Self-tuning experience-weighted attraction learning in games." Journal of Economic Theory, Vol. 133, 177-198.

Chmura, T., S., J., Goerg & R., Selten (2012) "Learning in Experimental 2 x 2 Games." Games and Economic Behavior, Vol. 76, No. 1 (September 2012): 44-73.

Selten, R., & J., Buchta (1999) "Experimental sealed bid first price auctions with directly observed bid functions." In D. Budescu, I. Erev, & R. Zwick (Eds.), Games and human behavior; essays in the honor of Amnon Rapoport, Hillsade. Erlbaum.

Ockenfels, A., & R., Selten (2005) " Impulse Balance Equilibrium and Feedback in First Price Auctions." Games and Economic Behavior, Vol. 51, pp. 155-170.

Avrahami, J., W., Güth & Y., Kareev (2005) "Games of Competition in a Stochastic Environment Theory and Decision, Vol. 59, No. 4, pp. 255-94.

Brunner, C., C., F., Camerer & J., K., Goeree (2001) "Stationary Concepts for Experimental 2x2 Games: Comment." The American Economic Review, Vol. 101, No. 2, pp. 1029-1040.

Selten, R., (ed.) (1991) Game Equilibrium Models I. Evolution and Game Dynamics, R. Selten Anticipatory learning in n-person games, Springer Verlag Berlin Heidelberg-New York 1991.

**Notes**

www.ingramcontent.com/pod-product-compliance
Lightning Source LLC
Chambersburg PA
CBHW062210220526
45470CB00009B/2997